MAY 2017

SandCastle

Word Families Set 7

-ook as in hook

Nancy Tuminelly

Consulting Editor Monica Marx, M.A./Reading Specialist

ABDO
Publishing Company

Published by SandCastle™, an imprint of ABDO Publishing Company, 4940 Viking Drive, Edina, Minnesota 55435.

Printed in the United States.

Credits
Edited by: Pam Price
Curriculum Coordinator: Nancy Tuminelly
Cover and Interior Design and Production: Mighty Media
Photo Credits: Comstock, Corbis Images, Digital Vision, Hemera, PhotoDisc, Stockbyte

Library of Congress Cataloging-in-Publication Data

Tuminelly, Nancy, 1952-
    -Ook as in hook / Nancy Tuminelly.
      p. cm. -- (Word families. Set VII)
    Summary: Introduces, in brief text and illustrations, the use of the letter combination "ook" in such words as "hook," "crook," "book," and "look."
    ISBN 1-59197-268-X
    1. Readers (Primary) [1. Vocabulary. 2. Reading.] I. Title. II. Series.

PE1119 .T828 2003
428.1--dc21
                                         2002038207

SandCastle™ books are created by a professional team of educators, reading specialists, and content developers around five essential components that include phonemic awareness, phonics, vocabulary, text comprehension, and fluency. All books are written, reviewed, and leveled for guided reading, early intervention reading, and Accelerated Reader® programs and designed for use in shared, guided, and independent reading and writing activities to support a balanced approach to literacy instruction.

Let Us Know

After reading the book, SandCastle would like you to tell us your stories about reading. What is your favorite page? Was there something hard that you needed help with? Share the ups and downs of learning to read. We want to hear from you! To get posted on the ABDO Publishing Company Web site, send us e-mail at:

sandcastle@abdopub.com

SandCastle Level: Transitional

-ook Words

book

brook

cook

crook

hook

look

Mary reads a book.

A duck swims in the
brook.

Em and her dad cook
dinner.

The police catch the crook.

Jo and her dad have a
fish on the hook.

Tracy is taking a closer look.

The Chef and the Cookbook

Jeff was a chef
who loved to cook.

One day he couldn't find
his cookbook.

Jeff looked for the book
in every nook.

Mr. Lee came by and said,
"Look what's on my hook!
This fish was in the brook."

Jeff the chef said, "I will cook what's on your hook when I find my cookbook."

In the door came a crook.

He said, "Hand over
what's on that hook."

Mr. Lee shook the hook,
and the crook took the fish
and Jeff's checkbook.

The crook did not look
when he dropped
the checkbook.

Jeff took his checkbook and bought a new cookbook.

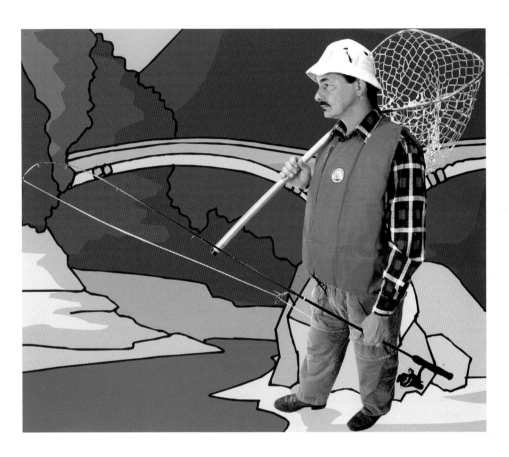

Mr. Lee went to the brook
to see what he could hook
for Jeff the chef to cook.

The -ook Word Family

book	look
brook	nook
checkbook	notebook
cook	rook
cookbook	shook
crook	took
hook	

Glossary

Some of the words in this list may have more than one meaning. The meaning listed here reflects the way the word is used in the book.

brook   a stream of water that is smaller than a river

crook   a person who is dishonest or has committed a crime

hook   a sharply curved piece of metal with a barb on the end that is used for catching fish

nook   a hidden or sheltered spot

About SandCastle™

A professional team of educators, reading specialists, and content developers created the SandCastle™ series to support young readers as they develop reading skills and strategies and increase their general knowledge. The SandCastle™ series has four levels that correspond to early literacy development in young children. The levels are provided to help teachers and parents select the appropriate books for young readers.

Emerging Readers
(no flags)

Beginning Readers
(1 flag)

Transitional Readers
(2 flags)

Fluent Readers
(3 flags)

These levels are meant only as a guide. All levels are subject to change.

ABDO
Publishing Company

To see a complete list of SandCastle™ books and other nonfiction titles from ABDO Publishing Company, visit www.abdopub.com or contact us at:

4940 Viking Drive, Edina, Minnesota 55435 • 1-800-800-1312 • fax: 1-952-831-1632